How the Camel got

A classic tale by Rudyard Kipling
Adapted by Gill Munton

Series Editor: Louis Fidge

Contents

How the Camel got his Hump

Camel lived in the desert.

When the world was new,
and the desert was new,
and the yellow, yellow sand was new,
Camel did not have a hump.

Yes, it's true! Camel did not have a hump!

But read the story and you will find out
how the Djinn of the Deserts
changed this in one week
and how Camel got his hump.

Chapter 1
Humph!

On the first Monday, the animals worked hard to help Man.

Man was their friend.

Horse carried Man on his back.

'Let's go, Horse!' said Man.

Dog fetched wood for him.

'Good Dog,' said Man.

Ox ploughed a field for him.

'Pull hard, Ox!' said Man.

But Camel was very lazy.
He did not want to work hard for Man.

He just wanted to stay in the desert.

He wanted to sleep in the sand.

He wanted to eat leaves.

When the other animals came to see him,
Camel opened one brown eye and said, 'Humph!'
Just 'Humph!' – and that was all.

Chapter 2

Horse

The other animals had a meeting.

'It's not fair!' said Ox.
'We do all the work.
Camel is very lazy.'

'He does not want to work,' said Dog.
'He just wants to stay in the desert.
He just wants to sleep and eat leaves.'

'You're right,' said Horse.
'It's not fair.
I will go to see that lazy Camel.
I will make him work!'

So Horse went to see Camel.

'Hello, Camel,' said Horse.

'Humph!' said Camel.

'You are very lazy,' said Horse.
'You do not want to work.
You just want to stay in the desert.
You just want to sleep and eat leaves.

Look at me.
I am Man's friend.
I carry him on my back.'

'Humph!' said Camel.

'Come on, Camel!' said Horse.
'Come with me.
Come to see Man.
Come to work with us.'

But Camel just said, 'Humph!'
Just 'Humph!' – and that was all.

So Horse went to see Man.

'I want to talk to you about Camel,' Horse said.
'He does not want to work.
He just wants to stay in the desert.
He just wants to sleep and eat leaves.

I carry you on my back.
Dog fetches wood for you.
Ox ploughs a field for you.
But Camel does nothing.
He just says, "Humph!"
Just "Humph!" – and that is all.'

'Thank you, Horse,' said Man.
'I will think about this.'

Chapter 3

Dog

On the first Tuesday, Dog said,
'I will go to see that lazy Camel.
I will make him work.'

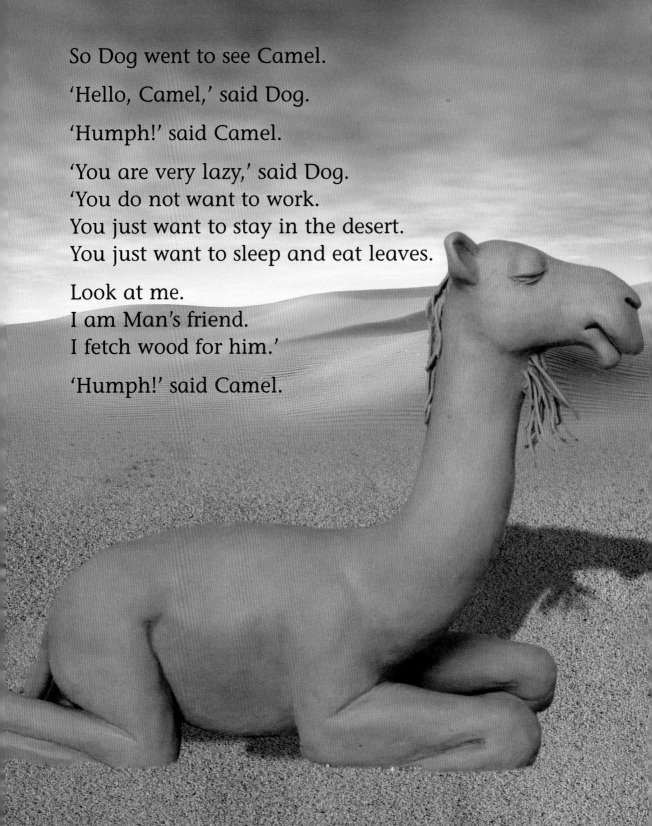

So Dog went to see Camel.

'Hello, Camel,' said Dog.

'Humph!' said Camel.

'You are very lazy,' said Dog.
'You do not want to work.
You just want to stay in the desert.
You just want to sleep and eat leaves.

Look at me.
I am Man's friend.
I fetch wood for him.'

'Humph!' said Camel.

'Come on, Camel!' said Dog.
'Come with me.
Come to see Man.
Come to work with us.'

But Camel just said, 'Humph!'
Just 'Humph!' – and that was all.

So Dog went to see Man.

'I want to talk to you about Camel,' Dog said.
'He does not want to work.
He just wants to stay in the desert.
He just wants to sleep and eat leaves.

I fetch wood for you.
Horse carries you on his back.
Ox ploughs a field for you.
But Camel does nothing.
He just says, "Humph!"
Just "Humph!" – and that is all.'

'Thank you, Dog,' said Man.
'I will think about this.'

Chapter 4

Ox

On the first Wednesday, Ox said,
'I will go to see that lazy Camel.
I will make him work.'

So Ox went to see Camel.

'Hello, Camel,' said Ox.

'Humph!' said Camel.

'You are very lazy,' said Ox.
'You do not want to work.
You just want to stay in the desert.
You just want to sleep and eat leaves.

Look at me.
I am Man's friend.
I plough a field for him.'

'Humph!' said Camel.

'Come on, Camel,' said Ox.
'Come with me.
Come to see Man.
Come to work with us.'

But Camel just said, 'Humph!'
Just 'Humph!' – and that was all.

So Ox went to see Man.

'I want to talk to you about Camel,' Ox said.
'He does not want to work.
He just wants to stay in the desert.
He just wants to sleep and eat leaves.

I plough a field for you.
Horse carries you on his back.
Dog fetches wood for you.
But Camel does nothing.
He just says, "Humph!"
Just "Humph!" – and that is all.'

'Thank you, Ox,' said Man.
'I will think about this.'

Chapter 5

The animals are angry

On the first Thursday, Man said to the animals,
'Camel is very lazy,
and he does not want to work.

So Horse, you work hard every day.
But you must work harder.
You must carry me to the town today.

So Dog, you work hard every day, too.
But you must work harder.
You must fetch lots of wood today.

'So Ox, you work hard every day, too.
But you must work harder.
You must plough three fields today.'

So Horse carried Man
to the town.

Dog fetched lots of wood
for him.

And Ox ploughed three
big fields for him.

In the evening, Horse said,
'I carried Man to the town.
It was a long way.'

'I fetched lots of wood for him,' said Dog.

'And I ploughed three fields for him,' said Ox.

The animals were very tired,
and they were very angry, too.

They went to see Camel.

'It's not fair,' said Horse.
'We do all the work, but you are very lazy.
You do not want to work.
You just want to stay in the desert.
You just want to sleep and eat leaves.'

But Camel just said, 'Humph!'
Just 'Humph!' – and that was all.

Chapter 6

The Djinn of the Deserts

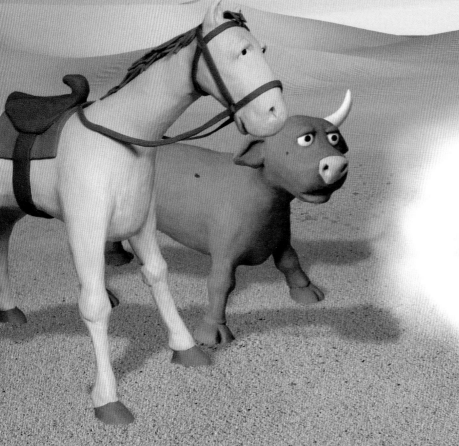

'Well,' said Horse. 'This is no good.
We do all the hard work.
But Camel does nothing.
Man will not help us.
He will not make Camel work.
What can we do?'

'I have got an idea!' said Dog.
'Let's call the Djinn of the Deserts.
The Djinn can do anything.
He will help us.'

So the animals called the Djinn of the Deserts.

They saw a white cloud and they heard
a *swish-swoosh* sound.

Next there was a big bang, and then the Djinn appeared.

'What do you want?' the Djinn asked.

'Our friend Camel is very lazy,' said Horse.
'We do all the work.
But Camel does nothing.
He won't carry Man on his back.'

'He won't fetch wood for him,' said Dog.

'And he won't plough fields for him,' said Ox.
'He just wants to stay in the desert.
He just wants to sleep and eat leaves
and say, "Humph!"
Do you think that's fair?'

'No, I don't think that's fair,' said the Djinn.
'I will go to see that lazy Camel.'

Then they saw the white cloud and they heard
the *swish-swoosh* sound.

Next there was a big bang,
and the Djinn was there no more.

So the Djinn went to see Camel.

Camel looked into a pool of water.
He saw his face and it made him laugh.

'You are very lazy, my friend,' said the Djinn.
'All the animals must help Man.'

'Humph!' said Camel.
Just 'Humph!' – and that was all.

Chapter 7

The magic hump

The Djinn sat down next to the pool.
He closed his eyes. He sat there for a long time.

'What are you doing?' asked Camel.
'Why are your eyes closed?'

'I am thinking hard,' said the Djinn.
'Turn your head and look at your back.'

Camel turned his head and looked at his back.
And there he saw a hump.

'What's *this*?' asked Camel.

'It's a humph,' said the Djinn.
'But you can call it a hump.'

'It is Thursday today,' said the Djinn.
'The other animals started work on Monday.
Now you are going to work, too.'

'But how can I work with this hump?'
asked Camel.

'The hump will help you,' said the Djinn.
'You have a lot of work to do.
There is food in the hump.

You won't have time to eat leaves.
You won't have time to sleep.
You won't have time to look at your face in the pool.
And you won't have time to say, "Humph!'"

'That's not fair!' said Camel.

'Oh yes, it is,' said the Djinn.
'Join the other animals.
Go to work for Man.'

Then Camel saw the white cloud,
and he heard the *swish-swoosh* sound.

Next there was a big bang,
and the Djinn was there no more.

Chapter 8

Camel carries Man

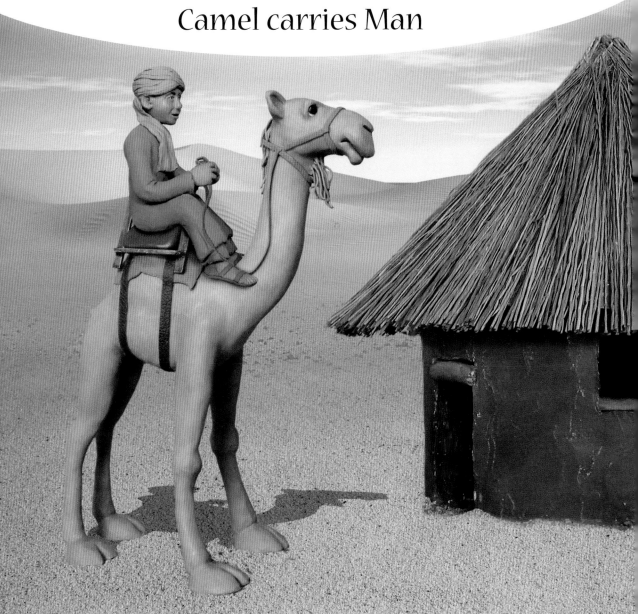

On the first Friday, Camel went to look for Man.
He wasn't happy.

'The Djinn told me to come,' he said to Man.

'Good,' said Man.
'You can carry me across the desert today.
I want to look at the sea.'

And so Man and Camel went across the desert.
It was a very long way.
Camel did not have time to eat leaves.

When they came to the sea,
Man looked at it and said,
'The world is new, Camel.
And the sea is new.
I just wanted to look at it.'

Man looked at the sea for a long time.

Then Man said, 'Let's go back now, Camel.'

So Man and Camel went back across the desert.
It was a very long way.
Camel did not have time to eat leaves.

In the evening, Camel was very tired.

'Tomorrow we will fetch wood,' said Man.

'Humph!' said Camel.

Chapter 9

Camel fetches wood

On the first Saturday, Man said,
'Come on, Camel!
We are going to fetch wood today.
I will cut down the trees.
You can pull the cart.'

And so Man and Camel went into the dark forest.

Man cut down some trees and put the wood in the cart.
Camel pulled the cart home.

Then they went to fetch more wood.
Camel did not have time to eat leaves.

In the evening, Camel was very tired.

'Tomorrow we will plough fields,' said Man.

'Humph!' said Camel.

Chapter 10

Camel ploughs fields

On the first Sunday, Man said,
'Come on, Camel!
We are going to plough fields today.
You can pull the plough.'

And so Man and Camel went to the fields.

Camel pulled the plough up and down, up and down.

He ploughed one field ... two fields ... three fields.
Camel did not have time to eat leaves.

In the evening, Camel was very tired.

'You worked very hard, Camel,' said Man.
'You carried me across the desert to the sea.
You fetched lots of wood for me.
You ploughed three fields for me.
Now you can eat leaves
and then you can sleep.'

'Humph!' said Camel.

So the Djinn of the Deserts
made Camel work at last!

And Camel still works today.

He still carries Man on his back.

He still fetches wood.

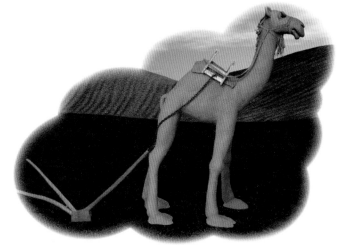

He still ploughs fields.

He still has his hump.

And he still ...

... says 'Humph!'

The Camel's Lament

Canaries feed on sugar and seed,
Parrots have crackers to crunch;
Horses eat hay and neigh all day,
And dogs munch bones for their lunch.
But I don't mind what food you bring,
A camel can eat anything!
ANYTHING does for me!

Cats fall asleep when they sit in a chair,
Puppies stay in their box;
Ponies are able to snooze in a stable,
And frogs doze all day on the rocks.
But a tired camel mustn't despair,
A camel can sleep anywhere!
ANY PLACE does for me!

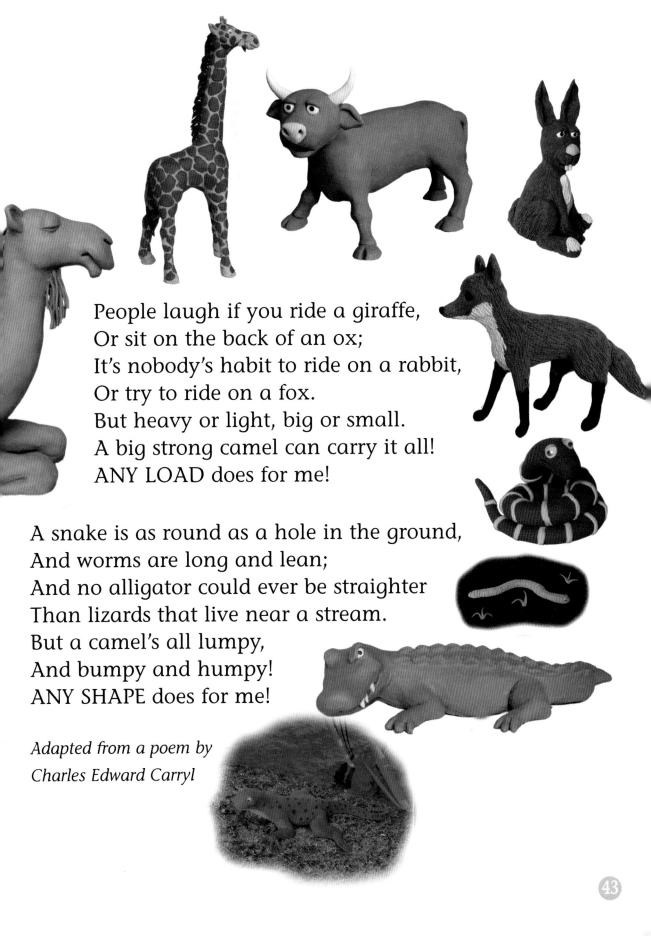

People laugh if you ride a giraffe,
Or sit on the back of an ox;
It's nobody's habit to ride on a rabbit,
Or try to ride on a fox.
But heavy or light, big or small.
A big strong camel can carry it all!
ANY LOAD does for me!

A snake is as round as a hole in the ground,
And worms are long and lean;
And no alligator could ever be straighter
Than lizards that live near a stream.
But a camel's all lumpy,
And bumpy and humpy!
ANY SHAPE does for me!

Adapted from a poem by
Charles Edward Carryl

43

The four animals in the story still work for man. Other animals work for man, too.

Dogs

Police dogs:
- catch criminals
- find guns and bombs
- find lost people
- find lost property
- help to control crowds.

Guide dogs help blind people to find their way.

Sheepdogs help shepherds to watch their sheep.

Guard dogs help guard buildings and scare thieves.

Sled dogs help to pull sledges across the snow and ice.

Camels, horses, oxen, donkeys and mules

These animals pull carts and ploughs. Horses also carry people on their backs.

Police horses help to control crowds.

Elephants

Elephants can pick up wood with their trunks.
They can also roll it along the ground.

Dolphins

Dolphins can work under the sea.

Pigeons

Pigeons can carry messages from one place to another.

All these animals help us.

We must help them, too.

We must make sure their lives are happy.

We must give them:
- kindness
- food, water and a home
- lots of rest
- treatment by a vet if they need it.

If you want to help lots of different animals all around the world, look at this interesting website: www.wspa-international.org

Macmillan Education
Between Towns Road, Oxford OX4 3PP
A division of Macmillan Publishers Limited
Companies and representatives throughout the world

ISBN 978-0-230-71986-6

Design and layout by Anthony Godber
Illustrated by Chris Petty
Cover design by Linda Reed and Associates
Cover illustration by in Chris Petty

The authors and publishers would like to thank the following
for permission to reproduce their photographic material:

Alamy/ Arco Images p45(t), Alamy/ Sally and Richard Greenhill
p44(c), Alamy/ Juniors Bildarchiv p44(br); Corbis/ Pennie Tweedie
p45(c); Getty/ Altrendo Images p44(bl); Photolibrary/ Digital Vision
p44(tr); Rex Features/ 45(b), Rex Features/ Michael Friedel p46(b),
Rex Features/ Jo Giordano p46(t); The Pigeon Archive 2007/
Richard Davies and Ståle Eriksen (Image courtesy the artist:
(www.lyndallphelps.com) p47.

Printed and bound in Malaysia

2014   2013   2012   2011   2010
10   9   8   7   6   5   4   3   2   1